G000058821

MUSIC AN
THE NATIONAL GALLERY OF IRELAND

Music and Paintings
in the
National Gallery of Ireland

Barra Boydell

THE NATIONAL GALLERY OF IRELAND 1985

British Library Cataloguing in Publication Data
Boydell, Barra
    Music and paintings in the National Gallery of
    Ireland
    1. Musical instruments in art   2. Painting
    I. Title   II. National Gallery of Ireland
    758'.978191   ND1460.M8

ISBN 0-903162-22-9

© Barra Boydell and the National Gallery of Ireland, 1985

First published, 1985, by the National Gallery of Ireland,
Merrion Square West, Dublin 2.

Edited by Joanna Mitchel and Adrian Le Harivel
Photography by Michael Olohan, Declan Emerson and John Kellett
Design, origination and print production by Printset and Design Ltd., Dublin

Printed in Ireland by Criterion Press Ltd.

Frontispiece: detail from *Love Triumphant,* attributed to Orazio Riminaldi.

Cover: detail from *Peasants Merrymaking* by David Teniers the Younger
and Lucas van Uden (Fig. 2).

Contents

Preface

OF THE TWO AND A half thousand or so oil paintings in the National Gallery of Ireland, a surprising number contain some musical allusion. Such allusions may take the form of an actual portrait of a musician (such as the portrait of the composer John Stevenson fig 74) or a figure portrayed with a musical instrument (as in the case of the striking *Portrait of Lady Mary Wortley-Montague* by Charles Jervas fig 26). Others contain musical intruments which are often included to convey a moral (as in the painting by de Keyser fig 56) or to accompany the singing of angels in religious scenes (for example the painting by del Biondo fig 33). The meaning that may be attached to such instruments is not always readily understood by the Gallery visitor, while the actual identity of the instruments themselves is more often than not only recognisable in the most general way. It is, however, apparent that the arts of music and painting have always been closely linked.

Barra Boydell is a music historian and he has looked at the paintings in the National Gallery, not from the point of view of their aesthetic appeal, but with regard to the references they make to music. He has found musical instruments in many paintings where they are subsidiary to the main themes of the picture. He has identified those instruments and in his text tells us how common they were at the time they were painted, the sounds which they made and how they differ from their modern day counterparts. He has looked at the Gallery's Collection with a new eye and his text will, I am sure, lead his readers to a fresher and keener appreciation of the many musical paintings in the National Gallery of Ireland.

His book is published in European Music Year and I hope it will encourage those who are interested in painting to an appreciation of music, and, by the same token, those who are interested in music to an enjoyment of painting.

Homan Potterton, *Director*
The National Gallery of Ireland, July 1985

Foreword

THIS BOOK PRESENTS a survey of the oil paintings in the National Gallery Collection which include musical instruments and musicians. It covers acquisitions up to 1981, excluding drawings, watercolours, miniatures, and sculpture. Other isolated paintings in which musicians might be present in small crowded details cannot be confirmed but these would not alter the overall view presented here. Since the Gallery can only display a part of the Collection at any one time, the paintings discussed here cannot be expected all to be on permanent show. However, the illustrations have been chosen with a view to showing the more significant musical features discussed. In some cases the musical content is so small and lacking in detail that it is not even very clear on the original and an illustration here would be of little use. In connection with this book, and as a contribution towards European Music Year 1985, a special exhibition of the more important paintings discussed here is being presented by the National Gallery of Ireland.

In presenting this survey of music in the paintings of the National Gallery it is hoped that this book will arouse an interest in the relationship between music and the visual arts and a keener visual awareness of the role of music in paintings, as well as contributing to the social history of music. It is also hoped that it will serve to introduce these paintings to students of music as well as of art history not only in this country but internationally.

I wish to record my sincerest thanks to the Director, Homan Potterton, and to the staff of the National Gallery, especially to Joanna Mitchel, for their help and co-operation while preparing this book.

Barra Boydell
Dublin, March 1985

1 *Music and Paintings*

SINCE EARLIEST TIMES people have portrayed themselves, their life and environment, their beliefs and superstitions, through paintings. At the same time music, of all the arts the most universal and central to our lives, has played a fundamental and central role in our artistic expression. The child singing as he plays, the adult humming as he walks, even the saturation of our lives by the background music of supermarkets and public places, all express our deeply felt, almost subconscious need for music at all levels of life; and this is not to count also the conscious seeking after musical experience by practicing musicians of all types and abilities, by concert goers, and by the listening public. On occasions of special ceremony too, the weddings and funerals of private life, the festivals and gatherings of public life, music is accepted even by those who make no pretence of being music-lovers as forming an essential element of the occasion.

It is therefore no surprise that music should be portrayed in paintings, whether directly in the form of singers and musicians or indirectly with musical instruments unplayed, since all paintings reflect the life and society of their times. Music appears in paintings in most periods in which the visual arts have flourished, to a degree which varies according to time and place not only because of the changing prominence of music at different periods, but also because artists have at times concentrated on aspects of society in which music did not play such a major role.

For students of the history of music and of musical instruments in particular paintings are of the greatest importance. A large part of our knowledge of the music and instruments of the more distant past is based on the visual arts. The archaeological records are slight, with few instruments surviving from earlier than the sixteenth century, and literary references, when they exist, normally at best tantalizingly ambiguous. In Egyptian tombs and on Greek vases we see musicians taking part in dances and in religious ceremonies, and from Roman times there are mosaics, reliefs, and even terra cotta figurines of musicians. Even when of subsidiary interest to the main subject of a painting, the role of music, the grouping of the types of instruments or singers, the way the instruments are held and the social context of their use, not to mention the date and place where the painting was done, all are of interest.

Music features in paintings in many different contexts. One of the oldest is religious art, for music has always been by its very nature close to man's spiritual expression in religion. Most European art in the Middle Ages was religious and it is here that we find from an early stage paintings of King David with his harp, the Elders of the Revelation with their instruments, or angel musicians in attendance on the Virgin Mary. Little by little secular music-making appears as non-religious subjects gain popularity in the Renaissance, first of all appearing as details in the background of religious paintings.

The Renaissance was distinguished from the preceeding centuries by the growing independence of life and society from the Church. The increased wealth of the merchant classes provided patronage for artists who now painted portraits and scenes reflecting everyday life as well as religious subjects. And so musical instruments and singers appear increasingly in scenes which reflect their place in contemporary life, in paintings of banquets, of dances, or of pageant and ceremony. At the same time many objects, including musical instruments, were used to convey an allegorical message which goes far deeper than a first glance at the painting might suggest. Sometimes too, musical instruments appear because their shape and colour make them visually appealing and appropriate to the composition of the painting.

The symbolism of musical instruments underlies much of their appearance in Renaissance and Baroque art, as well as their actual usage. Most significant was the relative acceptance of wind and stringed instruments. There was for a long time a prejudice against wind instruments related to their identification with sin and sensuality, especially in religious art. This is because, being blown directly by the player, wind instruments are more physical and sensual than

4

Plate 1. JACOPO VIGNALI *St. Cecilia.*

Plate 2. JEAN LEBEL *Fête Champêtre – Music.*

Plate 3. THOMAS COUTURE *Man Playing a Zampogna.*

Plate 4. CORNELIS TROOST *The Dilettanti.*

Plate 5. CHARLES JERVAS *Lady Mary Wortley-Montague with a Clavicytherium.*

Plate 6. JOSHUA REYNOLDS
*A Caricature: Thomas, 9th Earl of
Cassilis, Lord Charlemont,
Mr Ward and Mr Phelps.*

Plate 7.   detail from MARCO PALMEZZANO *The Virgin Enthroned with SS. John the Baptist and Lucy.*

Plate 8. NATHANIEL HONE THE ELDER *The Piping Boy.*

stringed instruments whose respectability was well established by the angels' association with the harp, the most ancient form of stringed instrument. The use of wind instruments in orgiastic rites in Ancient Greece is shown by the use of the aulos in Dionysian rites, while the god Pan is identified by the reed pipes which bear his name. In Renaissance art the shape of recorders, bagpipes and other wind instruments contributed to their use as phallic symbols, and many a painting of lovers includes a recorder or flute. In musical life the sixteenth century saw a gradual increase in the respectability of wind instruments, though still largely played by professional and itinerant musicians. No self-respecting lady or gentleman would wish to be seen playing an instrument which might distort his or her face with puffed out cheeks and a flushed countenance. Thus it was a long time before the reed and lip-reed instruments entered the realms of fashionable amateur music-making, the gentler flutes and recorders being the first to become socially acceptable. In France in the seventeenth century the aristocratic craze for a pastoral idyll was largely responsible for the development of the musette, a form of bagpipe on which, like on the uillean pipes, the mouth blown pipe is replaced by bellows, producing an admirably 'pastoral' instrument which could be played by ladies and gentlemen without upsetting their appearance.

It goes without saying that musical instruments in paintings must be examined closely before any conclusions can be drawn which may be significant from the musicological point of view. Even the most accurate draughtsman can produce musical nonsense when portraying a musician. Similar to the problem of painting galloping horses, which remained unsolved by artists until the invention of photography which could freeze the horse's movements, artists often experience difficulty in freezing musicians' movements in a way which is neither stilted nor unreal. Paintings of someone 'playing' an instrument may prove on closer inspection to show someone holding an instrument merely *as if* playing, the feeling of frozen movement lost in the prolonged pose in the artist's studio. More commonly, and this is where the artists who are musically experienced can be distinguished from those who are not, woodwind instruments in particular are shown being fingered in a way which is musical nonsense, but which an elementary understanding of how they are played would resolve.

Musical inaccuracies are not restricted to playing techniques.

5

Instruments which are acoustically or physically impossible abound and should arouse our suspicions enough to pause before using such paintings as historical evidence, though at the same time they need not necessarily be dismissed out of hand. On the one hand there are fantastic or imaginary instruments which represent their musical function without making any pretence at veracity. On the other hand are those which are physically impossible but which do not exclude the possibility that the artist had based his somewhat free instrument on a true model, the precise form of which we cannot know. Thus paintings provide for the music historian a record which must be evaluated with care. In the case of the reconstruction of mediaeval instruments for example we are largely dependent on visual records, and yet even then the most accurate representation can only show us the exterior of the instrument with little or no information as to such acoustically vital details as the bore of a wind instrument or the interior construction of a stringed instrument. We must also avoid the uncritical reproduction of a single representation of an instrument without establishing the degree to which it can be accepted as a model rather than being dismissed as the product of inadequate observation or artistic licence. Even the contexts and combinations of instruments in scenes of music-making cannot be accepted without question as the basis for historical performance hypotheses. In Dutch and Flemish seventeenth century paintings for example an ensemble of musicians may be determined by the demands of symbolism and not represent an actual musical ensemble at all. In fifteenth century paintings of the Virgin and Child whole 'orchestras' of angel musicians appear playing all manner of instruments. Again, this does not represent actual ensembles but is an expression of the angels praising the Virgin and Child 'with all manner of instruments'.

If paintings are of such great importance to the music historian despite the possible pitfalls outlined, it is also clear that the musical content of a painting can be of help to the art historian. Certain instruments can help in identifying the subject of an allegorical painting, the presence of a harp or a lira da braccio can identify the player in a mediaeval or renaissance painting as King David or as Apollo. The exact form of an instrument (provided that it can be accepted as an accurate portrayal) can help in identifying the date or provenance of a painting, and fakes have even been identified by the presence of a totally anachronistic musical instrument in a painting supposedly by an earlier artist.

The National Gallery of Ireland has built up its Collection over a period of more than a century, covering a wide range of schools and periods. Paintings have been acquired, bequeathed or sought out, for various reasons not involving the musical content which any of the paintings may have. Thus the musical content can be regarded, as in any comparable collection, as arbitrary and as such, as representing a more or less random and representative cross-section of the role of music in the schools represented in the Collection. Thus the fine collection of Dutch and Flemish paintings is reflected in the larger number of paintings of musical interest, while the much smaller number of paintings with music from the German school, for example, reflects the relative size of that school in the Gallery. Taken as a whole this essentially random selection of musical paintings provides a fine selection of the types of European paintings in which music occurs and the role it plays in them, while at the same time including some outstanding individual works.

Fig. 1. PIETER BRUEGHEL THE YOUNGER. *A Peasant Wedding*, dated 1620.

2 Music and Life

PAINTINGS OF SCENES from daily life at all levels of society include musicians and reflect the social and musical contexts of music-making, showing what instruments were played at different periods, by whom and in what settings. Often the most important paintings in this category are those in which musicians play a subsidiary role but nevertheless appear in their natural context. By contrast, a portrait or a still-life may feature instruments out of their musical context and chosen for what they represent rather than for purely musical reasons.

Fig. 1a. detail.

In paintings of rural life music features especially in the 17th century Dutch and Flemish schools. Pieter Brueghel the Younger, son of the more famous painter of the same name, copied or closely followed many of his father's paintings. *A Peasant Wedding* (fig 1), dated 1620, shows a wedding feast in a barn. The bride is seated at a table while guests contribute, not without argument, to her dowry. Couples embrace and others dance to the music of two bagpipers (fig 1a detail) who stand at the back of the room. With the greed and wrath of the argument over the dowry, and the lust of the embracing couples, this painting is as much a moral allegory as a straightforward scene of peasant merrymaking. In this respect the presence of the bagpipes has a significance beyond their musical and social appropriateness to the scene, since bagpipes are often imbued with a deliberate phallic meaning in paintings of this period. Bagpipes like these also occur in many pictures by other artists, normally with a conical chanter with a wide bell and two long, slender cylindrical drones, but no examples of this type, once so widespread throughout Northern Europe, are known to survive. Frequently one drone was longer than the other, the two being tuned a fifth apart, but in this painting they are similar in length. A

9

Fig. 2.   DAVID TENIERS THE YOUNGER with LUCAS VAN UDEN. *Peasants Merrymaking.*   *Fig. 2a.*   detail.

solitary bagpiper accompanies two couples dancing out of doors in a painting of *Peasants Merrymaking* (fig 2) by David Teniers the Younger with Lucas Van Uden. Here the bagpipe has one drone much longer than the other and the chanter, though slightly conical, has no expanded bell.

Tavern scenes, especially out of doors, are a rich source of music in paintings. There are often people dancing, accompanied by one or more musicians. An unusually large ensemble appears in Gerrit Lundens' *A Village Merrymaking* (fig 3). One of the four musicians plays a bagpipe similar to that in Brueghel's painting but with only one drone pipe. A second plays a large shawm, the ancestor of the modern oboe, while a third plays another wind instrument which, though largely hidden, looks like a second shawm. They are accompanied by a drummer.

10

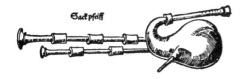

Fig. 2b. **Bagpipes,** from SEBASTIAN VIRDUNG. *Musica Getutscht,* (Basel, 1511).

Fig. 3. GERRIT LUNDENS. *A Village Merrymaking.*

Instruments which accompany themselves with a continuous drone, of which the bagpipe is the most familiar, occur in the folk music of many countries. An equivalent stringed instrument is the hurdy-gurdy whose ancestry dates back to the early Middle Ages and which was especially associated during the 17th century in France and the Low Countries with itinerant and pauper musicians (fig 4). On the hurdy-gurdy the strings are sounded not by a bow but by a rosined wheel which is turned by a cranked handle at one end of the instrument and which produces an uninterrupted sound. Two or more strings sound a continuous drone, while the tune is played by pressing down keys. A hurdy-gurdy is shown in *A Tavern Scene* by Cornelis Dusart (fig 4) dated 1692. The solo musician here, a child or a dwarf, holds his large hurdy-gurdy under his left arm, fingers on the keys, and turns the handle to sound the strings with his right hand.

Moving indoors, a painting by Cornelis Bega dated 1662 shows *Two Men Singing* (fig 5) from a sheet of music in a room full of clutter. In the foreground rests a large four-stringed violoncello. During the

Fig. 4. CORNELIS DUSART. *A Tavern Scene*, dated 1692.

Fig. 4a. detail.

seventeenth century this bass member of the violin family, sometimes known as *basse de violon,* occurred in a variety of sizes and with four, five, or even six strings. It was only towards the end of the century that the smaller, four-stringed form which we recognise as the cello began to predominate.

Jean Marchand's *Cabaret Scene in Damascus* (fig 6), painted in the early part of this century, shows a more modern and exotic musical group, a sword swallower accompanied by six large frame drums. The frame drum, on which the diameter of the head is considerably greater than the depth of the wooden sides, is one of the oldest forms of drum. The best known form is the tambourine, distinguished by its metal jingles or bells around the sides, while the Irish *bodhrán* (fig 7) is another form.

In marked contrast to the social milieu of the foregoing paintings, fashionable music-making out of doors is epitomised by the French '*fêtes*

Fig. 4b. **Hurdy-Gurdy** by JOHN QUIG, Coleraine late 18th century. *National Museum of Ireland.*

12

Fig. 5. CORNELIS BEGA. *Two Men Singing,* dated 1662.

Fig. 6. JEAN MARCHAND. *Cabaret Scene in Damascus.*

Fig. 7. **Bodhrán, Co. Limerick c.1940.**
Photo Kevin Danagher.

Fig. 8.   JEAN LEBEL. *Fête Champêtre – Music.*

champêtres' of the 18th century. In their pursuit of an idealised pastoral life
the aristocracy adopted and made fashionable many things associated
with rural life, including musical instruments. Amongst these was the
hurdy-gurdy which, as we have seen, was formerly associated with the
lowest level of society. A hurdy-gurdy is played in one of a pair of *fêtes
champêtres* (fig 8) by Jean Lebel. An elegant couple is dancing, watched by
others resting in the shade of the trees, and in the background a
musician plays, only his hand turning the crank handle and part of the

Fig. 8a.   **Flute** by P.J. BRESSAN, London c.1710.
Victoria and Albert Museum, London.

16

Fig. 9. JEAN LEBEL. *Fête Champêtre – Dance.*

belly of the instrument being visible. In the second painting by Lebel (fig 9) a larger number of musicians, possibly aristocratic amateurs, are playing and singing. On the right are two violinists (both violins look large and so could be violas), and on the left in a group around a seated lady two gentlemen sing and another plays a flute. The (fig 8a) flute enjoyed great popularity in the 18th century especially amongst amateurs and is often found in association with pastoral music because of its origins in shepherds' pipes. Flutes appear in a number of other

Fig. 10. JEAN-BAPTISTE PATER. *Fête Champêtre.*

paintings in the National Gallery, in particular in Cornelis Troost's *The Dilettanti* (fig 24, see Chapter 3). The flute in Lebel's painting, of pale wood (typically boxwood) with ivory or silver mounts and single key not clear in the painting, is characteristic of the period. Two ladies behind the seated lady may be singing, though this is uncertain.

Another two *fêtes champêtres* by the early 18th century painter Jean-Baptiste Pater also include musicians. In one (fig 10) a couple dances to the music of a violin and a musette. Just as the hurdy-gurdy had become fashionable in 18th century France, so too had the bagpipe, but in the form of the musette which is blown with bellows and not with the mouth (fig 10a). It thus does not require great physical effort to play nor does it distort the players face by blowing and it was therefore

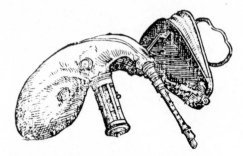

Fig. 10a. **Musette** from MICHAEL PRAETORIUS, *Syntagma Musicum II, De Organographia,* (Wolfenbüttel, 1619-1620.)

Fig. 11. **Follower of** ANTOINE WATTEAU. *A Music Party (Le Conteur).*

Fig. 12. GIOVANNI PASSERI. *A Party Feasting in a Garden.*

considered appropriate for elegant society. Giovanni Passeri's *A Party Feasting in a Garden* (fig 12), an Italian painting of the mid 17th century, shows music accompanying an outdoor meal. A youth stands behind the diners playing a guitar and one of the ladies at the table plays a tambourine. The guitar (fig 13a) had spread from its native Spain throughout much of Europe during the preceding century but it was

19

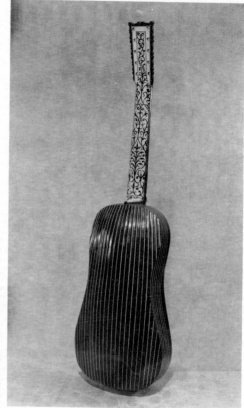

Fig. 13a. **Guitar,** Italian mid 17th century.
Victoria and Albert Museum, London.

Fig. 13. After DAVID TENIERS THE YOUNGER.
A Music Party Out of Doors.

especially popular in Italy, taking over the role that had formerly been held by the lute in amateur music-making.

A contemporary painting after David Teniers the Younger, *A Music Party Out of Doors* (fig 13), shows people playing music on a terrace. A young man sings from a music book, a lady is seated at a table possibly also singing, and they are accompanied by a lady playing a plucked instrument which is mostly hidden except for the pegbox which

Fig. 14. Attributed to GERRIT VAN HONTHORST. A Wedding Feast, dated 1628.

Fig. 14a. **Lute,** from MICHAEL PRAETORIUS, *Syntagma Musicum II, De Organographia,* (Wolfenbüttel, 1619-1620).

suggests a guitar, and a man playing a six stringed *basse de violon.* On the balustrade behind the musicians sits a monkey, a symbol of vice, suggesting that the painting conceals a meaning which goes beyond the apparently innocuous music party it appears to be.

Music-making indoors features in a number of paintings. In the Renaissance this is often in the context of biblical scenes portrayed in contemporary settings, as in Francken's *Marriage Feast at Cana* (fig 39) in

Fig. 15.   HENDRICK DE HONDT. *An Interior of a Guardroom.*

which the setting is a late 16th century Flemish banquet, complete with musicians on a balcony (see Chapter 4). Another *Wedding Feast* on a more intimate scale is dated 1628 and is attributed to Gerrit van Honthorst (fig 14). The bride and bridegroom sit at a table, entertained by a man who sings to the accompaniment of his lute.

    Music has always formed part of military life, trumpets and drums being used for fanfares, for signalling in battle, and for marching. A 15th century Florentine painting of *The Taking of Pisa* (fig 16) includes amongst many figures in the battle scene a pipe and tabor player and a trumpeter (detail, fig 16a), while a 17th century Dutch painting, *An Interior of a Guardroom* by Hendrick de Hondt (fig 15), shows a drum and trumpet amongst other military equipment. In Francis Wheatley's large painting

Fig. 16.   FLORENTINE SCHOOL, (15th CENTURY). *The Taking of Pisa in 1406,* dated 1440.

Fig. 16a.   detail.

of *The Dublin Volunteers in College Green, Dublin, 4th November 1779* (fig 17) the drummer appropriate to such a gathering is visible in the front of the other soldiers (fig 17a detail). A full cavalry band appears in a painting by Turner de Lond (See Chapter 6).

There is a pair of paintings of palatial interiors by the late 18th century Austrian artist Matthias Schiffer. One of these, *An Interior with a Fancy Dress Ball in Progress* (fig 18) includes the musicians one would expect to find in any scene of a ball or dance, but in this painting so small and insignificant a part of the whole painting that they might easily be overlooked. They were added in after the background had been completed and are so lightly painted that they seem like ghosts, with the wall and pilasters visible through them. The type of ensemble shown might be associated with the serenades and divertimenti of Mozart and Haydn. Indeed, with the late 18th century Austrian setting these musicians could even be playing Mozart or Haydn's music. The instrumentation is mixed, consisting of both wind and strings: two oboes, two horns, two bassoons (or by their small size possibly *fagottini,* tenor bassoons which existed parallel to the normal bass instrument well into the 19th century), three violins (or possibly violas), and a double bass.

Paintings in the National Gallery which show music in 19th century life are mainly associated with Ireland and are discussed in a later chapter.

Fig. 17.　FRANCIS WHEATLEY. *The Dublin Volunteers in College Green, 4th November, 1779.*

Fig. 17a.　detail.

Fig. 18. MATTHIAS SCHIFFER. *An Interior with a Fancy Dress Ball in Progress,* dated 1777.

Fig 18a. detail.

3 Portraits

MUSICAL INSTRUMENTS APPEAR in several portraits in the National Gallery. In some cases this is because the sitter is a musician and is shown with the tools of his trade, but in others the presence of musical instruments is used to enhance the sitter's cultural reputation, to indicate that his or her cultural education includes music-making. These portraits with musical instruments are often of particular interest from an organological point of view because of the detail and prominence with which instruments may be depicted.

Portraits of musicians in the National Gallery include Francis Bindon's painting and engraving of the great 18th century Irish harper *Turlough O'Carolan* (fig 57) with his harp (which however is only partially shown), Conn O'Donnell's portrait of the harper Art O'Neill (fig 58), and three examples from the 19th century of bagpipe players: from Ireland there are two players of uillean pipes, Joseph Haverty's *The Blind Piper* (fig 64) and Thomas Bridgford's *An Irish Piper* (fig 65). A quite different type of bagpipe appears in Thomas Couture's *Man Playing a Zampogna*, (fig 19) which shows the zampogna which is a form of bagpipe native to southern Italy and Sicily but often played in the past by itinerant musicians who used to travel throughout Europe. This painting realistically conveys the piper's concentration and effort as he plays, seated on a bench against a plain background. The most characteristic feature of the zampogna, clear in this painting, is its two long chanters with expanded bells, one fingered by each hand. These are tuned to different pitches so that melodies can be played in two parts, accompanied by the drones which have shorter pipes (fig 19a).

Undoubtedly the finest portrait of a musician, and one of the gems of the whole Gallery, is the late 15th century *Portrait of a Musician* (fig 20)

Fig. 19a. **Zampogna,** ITALIAN 19th CENTURY. *Pitt Rivers Museum, Oxford.*

Fig. 19. THOMAS COUTURE.
Man playing a Zampogna,
dated 1877.

Fig. 20. Attributed to FILIPPINO LIPPI.
Portrait of a Musician.

28

attributed to Filippino Lippi. A man dressed in black is tuning a lira da braccio, while on shelves behind him lie sheets of music and other musical instruments: a lute, a second lira da braccio with its bow, and two small wind instruments, probably recorders. During the later 15th century Italian courts were increasingly concerned with the patronage of the arts as a reflection of their magnificence, creating a climate in which music flourished. It is more than likely that this is a portrait of one of the highly acclaimed poet-musicians of the period, men like Pietrobono who was attached to the d'Este court at Ferrara and whose fame spread throughout Italy. The inscription in the lower corner, in the Ferrarese dialect, reads *e ichonjcar no fia p tempo mai* ('and it will never be too early to begin'); this could be a quotation from a poem or song written by the sitter.

With its four or five melody strings (not visible here, but five pegs can be seen in the pegbox) and characteristic drone string running from the side of the pegbox and held in this case by a finely carved peg in the form of a hand, the lira da braccio was considered the noblest solo instrument of the period in Italy and was widely used to accompany the recitation of epic and narrative poetry (fig 20a). The esteem in which it was held was enhanced by the belief that it was the 'lyre' of the god Apollo and of Orpheus, both of whom are frequently portrayed in contemporary paintings with this instrument. Certainly, the noble association of the lira da braccio and the richly carved decoration of the instrument in this painting show that this is not the portrait of a common musician.

A man tuning a stringed instrument is also the subject of *A Violinist* dated 1645 (fig 21) by Godart Kamper. Coincidentally the young man here is also dressed in black, in the Dutch fashion of his day. He sits beside a table on which rest books, one of which is open, the pages hidden to view but presumably containing music. He is tuning the top string of his violin which, although largely hidden by his right forearm, displays the characteristic features of the time including the short and relatively flat fingerboard of pale-coloured wood. At this time the violin was beginning to establish for itself the pre-eminent position which it has maintained ever since.

A portrait by Jan Mytens of *A Lady Playing A Lute* (fig 23) is dated 1648 and features the lute as an accessory enhancing the sitter's cultural standing. The lady is playing a 'theorbed' lute. During the

Fig. 20a. **Lira da Braccio,** by GIOVANNI MARIA. Brescia, Italy 1st half of 16th century. *Ashmolean Museum, Oxford.*

Fig. 22.   After ANTHONY VAN DYCK. *The Concert.*

Fig. 21.   GODART KAMPER. *A Violinist,* dated 1645.

16th and 17th centuries the lute was fashionable amongst cultured amateurs and this form, especially favoured by French lute composers and thus known in England as the 'French lute', has two distinct pegboxes (fig 22a). The main pegbox is angled sharply back from the neck in the normal manner and in addition there is a smaller pegbox which continues the line of the neck and carries the lowest strings,

Fig. 23. JAN MYTENS, *A Lady Playing a Lute,* dated 1648.

Fig. 22a. **Theorboed Lute,** by JONAS STEHELIN, (Strassburg, 1596). *Karl-Marx Universität, Leipzig.*

open bass strings which are not fingered. It is interesting to note in Mytens' painting that, in spite of the artist's apparent attention to detail the number of strings does not correspond with the number of pegs, and the pegs themselves are painted somewhat randomly. In addition to reflecting the sitter's cultural aspirations, the lute in this painting may serve a secondary function: in contemporary emblematic

Fig. 24. CORNELIS TROOST. *The Dilettanti,* dated 1736.

literature the lute appears as an emblem of temperence, an attribute most appropriate for the lady in the portrait. Another lute played by a lady, also from the mid-seventeenth century, appears in *The Concert* after a painting by Van Dyck, which is a double portrait in an outdoor setting (fig 22).

The fashionable and possibly too the symbolic aspects of musical instruments recur in another Dutch portrait of the early 18th century,

GEORGE BROWN Musical Instrument Maker, dwelling at Mr. Hyena's, Cutler in Crane-lane, Dublin, has by his Skill and Industry, brought that Instrument called the German Flute to that Degree of Perfection, that the most Knowing in that Art can find no Defect in them, and by a new Machine of his own Invention, Gentlemen may with the greatest Facility found all the Notes of the said Instrument, from the highest to the lowest. He also makes excellent German Cane Flutes, for the Accommodation of those Gentlemen that would recreate themselves abroad and as he has been for this considerable Time past a successful Practitioner in his Art, and has wrought for the most eminent Masters in his Travels through Germany, Holland, Flanders and England, humbly hopes, Gentlemen such as have occasion for said Instrument will favour him with their Custom, and they may be assured of getting good Instruments from him as is possible to be made.

Fig. 24a. Advertisement by GEORGE BROWN, flute-maker, from *The Dublin Courant*, January 16th-19th, 1747. *National Library of Ireland.*

Cornelis Troost's *The Dilettanti* (fig 24). This shows the Amsterdam merchant Jeronimus Tonneman and his son and is dated 1736. Father and son are sitting at a table, the son playing a flute. While the lute had been the fashionable instrument at the time Mytens was painting, its place was taken in the 18th century by the flute. During the later 17th century, in common with other woodwind instruments, it underwent profound changes in design resulting in a considerably more expressive and versatile instrument which rapidly gained popularity, reflected in the immense amount of music published for the instrument. King Frederick the Great of Prussia is perhaps the most famous amateur flautist of the 18th century. Troost's painting thus shows the flute in its fashionable setting, the instrument shown being an up-to-date flute of the time, with its single key and four-piece construction, while the silver mountings and the slim and elegant profile suggest quality and expense. And yet this painting, for all its air of cultural refinement, hints too at the former association of the flute and other woodwind instruments in the art of the Renaissance and early Baroque as an erotic symbol. A year after this picture was painted the flautist, the younger Tonneman, stabbed his mistress, who had born him a child, with a scissors. Did the younger Tonneman simply wish to be portrayed as cultured and fashionable playing his flute, or was Troost hinting at the darker side of his character perhaps already evident at the time by showing him with a flute whose symbolism may not have been entirely forgotten by then? Certainly the partially visible relief above the fireplace suggests an element of wit, for it shows Mercury killing Argus, which he did having first lulled Argus to sleep by playing a pipe.

One of the most influencial performers and composers of the late 17th and early 18th centuries was the Italian violinist Arcangelo Corelli who had a major influence on the development of music for strings, in particular for the violin. The National Gallery has a portrait of *Corelli* (fig 25) by the Irish painter Hugh Howard. Howard painted at least three similar portraits of Corelli whom he must have met while in Rome between 1697 and 1700, but this example is unique in including a surround of music and musical instruments. In the foreground lie two violins and a book of music which shows on the left the opening bars of Corelli's Trio Sonata opus 3 no 7. The music on the right page is the opening of the second movement (Allegro) of his Sonata opus 5 no 6 for solo violin and continuo, published in 1700.

Two 18th century portraits with Irish connections can be singled out for their musical interest. The large portrait of *Lady Mary Wortley Montague with a Clavicytherium* (fig 26) by Charles Jervas who was born in County Offaly in 1675 and worked both in Ireland and in England, includes a free representation of a clavicytherium or upright harpsichord. Whereas in the portraits discussed above the sitters were actively involved with their instruments, whether tuning or playing them, here the lady is standing beside a musical instrument, one hand

Fig. 25. HUGH HOWARD. *Arcangelo Corelli,* (1653-1713).

Fig. 26. CHARLES JERVAS. *Lady Mary Wortley-Montague with a Clavicytherium, (1689-1762).*

Fig. 26a. **Clavicytherium,** by JOHN ROTHER, Dublin mid 18th century. *National Museum of Ireland.*

resting lightly on the keyboard, but with no suggestion that she is going to play it. The clavicytherium acts here as a cultural prop rather than as an extension of the sitter's personality, while also contributing significantly to the composition of the painting.

Upright harpsichords have existed since an early stage in the development of the instrument in the late Middle Ages. The upright form enjoyed a vogue during the 18th century, and some are known to have been made in Dublin, an example by Henry Rother surviving in the National Museum of Ireland (fig 26a). The instrument in Jervas's painting however is of a very unusual form copied from a painting dated c.1640 by the Italian artist Andrea Sacchi, now in the Metropolitan Museum of Art in New York (fig 27), which depicts Apollo crowning the famous castrato Marc Antonio Pasqualini. Pasqualini's character is enhanced by many allegorical symbols including the instrument upon which he rests his hand. It is identical to and explains many unusual features on the instrument in Jervas's painting. Most noticeable is the impossible weakness of the frame of Jervas's instrument. The considerable strain of the strings is supported by a slender rail parallel to the keyboard and by the no less fragile arms of a carved female figure on the right side of the frame, above which the slightest of garlands connects with the pedimented top of the instrument.

Much of the symbolism in Sacchi's painting is concerned with the triumph of intelligence and truth, and the triumph of control over passion. The decoration on the clavicytherium, with the female figure and garland and the leaves above the keyboard, alludes to the story of Daphne and Apollo. Pursued by Apollo, the chaste nymph Daphne prayed to be transformed. Her plea was answered and she was changed into a laurel tree, which Apollo then adopted as a symbol of his esteem for her. Thus the story of Daphne and Apollo symbolises the triumph of chastity over passion. On the instrument in Sacchi's painting the figure of Daphne changing into a laurel wreath is substantial enough to fulfil its structural role as part of the instrument. Jervas's painting was not copied directly from Sacchi but at one remove from a portrait by Godfrey Kneller, whom he succeeded as principal painter to King George I in 1723, of Elizabeth Churchill, Countess of Bridgewater, now in a private collection in England. In Kneller's painting the laurel wreath is already less substantial, but not to the

Fig. 27. ANDREA SACCHI. *Apollo Crowning the Castrato Marc Antonio Pasqualini,* (1614-1691), dated 1640. *Metropolitan Museum of Art, New York.*

impossible degree shown by Jervas. The classical form of the frame pillar on the left of the instrument and the pediment on top emphasise the classical allusions in Sacchi's painting, while the quite unusual dolphin legs of Jervas's instrument, of which only one is visible, also have their antecedents with Sacchi who shows three such legs, a reference to the classical symbolism of the tripod representing truth in association with the oracle of Apollo.

Thus the clavicytherium in Jervas's painting represents a degenerate copy of a largely symbolic instrument in an earlier painting, the symbolical significance of the original having been lost. But this is compounded by the fact that Jervas did not have a good understanding of musical principles, so that for example the keyboard shows some black keys placed in the middle of a white key rather than between them, and the top of the keys themselves are untypically convex. There is however isolated evidence for clavicytheria of the general type represented, with the rare feature of the soundboard not behind the strings but below them. The most important is a description and illustration in Mersenne's *Harmonie Universelle* of 1636-7, in which this type of instrument is significantly associated with Rome, where Sacchi worked.

This painting typifies one of the main difficulties in musical iconography, the extent to which instruments can be accepted as depicted. In this case, the fortunate survival of the original model for the instrument shown by Jervas explains many of its unusual features, although the question still remains as to the extent to which Sacchi himself may have been inventing certain details rather than depicting an actual instrument.

The second 18th century painting of Irish interest features instruments not as mere props but being enthusiastically played. This is a character group by Sir Joshua Reynolds (fig 28) which repeats with some alterations one of the groups of figures in his *Parody on Raphael's School of Athens*, also in the National Gallery. In the smaller painting three gentlemen play flute, recorder, and cello, while a fourth looks on. Reynolds painted this group while in Rome in 1751 and it portrays various people who were visiting Rome in the course of the Grand Tour. The recorder player is the Irish peer Lord Charlemont, whose Dublin townhouse is now the Hugh Lane Municipal Gallery in Parnell Square and who built the Casino at Marino, Fairview. The flautist is the 9th Earl of Cassilis who, as a Scotsman, wears a thistle in his hat, and the cellist, the Welshman Mr. Phelps, wears a leek. The onlooker behind is Mr Ward, an Englishman.

The players show all the enthusiasm and enjoyment of amateur music-making, probably as they met at the house of Pier Leone Ghezzi, a keen amateur musician and painter himself who was on close terms with cultivated society and organised an association for informal

Fig. 28. JOSHUA REYNOLDS. *A Caricature: Thomas, 9th Earl of Cassilis, Lord Charlemont, Mr Ward and Mr Phelps,* painted 1751.

music-making in Rome. The combination of instruments provides a typical group for baroque trio sonatas, but without the harpsichord, the two upper instruments, here flute and recorder, and the bass line played by the cello, forming a musical whole in the trio sonata.

Portraits of Irish musicians of more recent date are discussed in

Fig. 29. ANGELICA KAUFFMAN. *The Earl of Ely and his Family,* dated 1771.

Chapter 6, but remaining in the 18th century there are a number of further portraits from other countries in which musical instruments occur. Angelica Kauffman's large portrait of the *Earl of Ely and his Family* (fig 29) includes his niece, Dolly Monroe, seated at the harpsichord with the artist herself standing nearby. The instrument is largely hidden, but on the music stand rests a book of music open at an Italian aria from *La Buona Figliuola* by Niccolo Piccini. It is worth noting that Angelica Kauffman was herself an accomplished musician.

Sometimes musical instruments occur in portraits as one of many objects either in the background or adjacent to the sitter, as in other 18th century portraits in the Gallery. For example there is a harpsichord in the backgrounds of Jan Vierpyl's presumed portrait of *Francis Hutcheson the Philosopher with his Daughter,* dated 1721 (fig 30), and in the group portrait of *The Western Family* by William Hogarth (fig 32) (in which the harpsichord is back to front, the bass strings are on the instrument's right and the shorter treble strings are on the left!). The

Fig. 30. JAN VIERPYL. *A Presumed Portrait of Francis Hutcheson (1694-1746) with his Daughter,* dated 1721.

Fig. 31. ALEXANDRE ROSLIN. *Le Marquis de Vaudreuil (1724-1802),* painted c.1759.

lid of the harpsichord in Vierpyl's painting is painted on the inside in the Flemish and French tradition, while the harpsichord in Hogarth's painting has an undecorated lid in the English style.

An example in which instruments are selected amongst other objects to reflect facets of the sitter's character without being singled out to the extent of being held or played is Alexandre Roslin's portrait of the *Marquis de Vaudreuil* (fig 31): on a table beside the Marquis lie pens, paper, an open book and a violin, of which only the neck and head is visible, with its bow.

Fig. 32. WILLIAM HOGARTH. *The Western Family,* dated 173-?.

4 *Cecilia, Saints, and Sinners*

RELIGIOUS ART HAS for many centuries been the predominant form of western art. At the same time music has had a long and often complex relationship with the Christian Church. Old Testament exhortations to praise God with music and descriptions of angel musicians were counterbalanced by the role of music, especially instrumental music, in dancing and other worldly pleasures which the Church condemned. Attitudes changed in this delicate balance between the acceptability and the sinfulness of music from one period to another, and from one country to another, changes inevitably reflected in religious art. While vocal music was most often acceptable because of its close association with angelic choirs, the position of musical instruments was less secure. Wind instruments for example have often been seen as symbols of vice and debauchery, and their appearance in religious art is frequently related to such symbolism.

One of the earliest instruments to appear in religious art is the harp, played by King David, by the angels, or by the twenty-four elders of the Revelation. The respectability thus accorded to the harp was extended to cover most other stringed instruments, a respectability paralleled in the Renaissance when the interest in classical mythology showed stringed instruments associated with Apollo, who represented the civilised side of man's nature, while Bacchus and Dionysius, representing the passionate and sensual side, were associated with pipes and other wind instruments.

During the late Middle Ages musical instruments begin to appear played by angels accompanying the Virgin and Child or at the birth of Christ. The National Gallery has a 14th century painting by Giovanni del Biondo of the *Virgin and Child with Angel Musicians* (fig 33) in which

Fig. 33. GIOVANNI DEL BIONDO. *The Virgin and Child with Angel Musicians.*

Fig. 33a.   detail.

the Virgin is seated on a dias, holding the Child Jesus and flanked by angels. God the Father watches from above and in front kneel two angel musicians. One plays a six stringed vielle or mediaeval fiddle, the leading bowed instrument of cultured music-making at the time. The second angel plays a small portative organ with a single row of ten pipes. Small organs like this, which could be carried by the player and hence the term 'portative', were widely used especially in art music.

43

Fig. 34. MARCO PALMEZZANO. *The Virgin Enthroned with SS. John the Baptist and Lucy,* dated 1513.

Fig. 34a. detail.

The player worked a small bellows with one hand, leaving the other free to play a single line of music. From its beginnings as an instrument of circus and spectacle in Ancient Rome the organ had established for itself a certain respectability earlier in the Middle Ages, although the larger instruments used in churches and cathedrals were cumbersome compared to the more familiar instruments which later developed. However, especially in the small 'portative' form, it did not yet have the almost exclusive association with the Church which it later gained.

During the 15th century the practice of including instruments in religious paintings grew more widespread. Whole choirs and orchestras of angels playing virtually all known instruments of the time occur, answering the biblical exhortation to praise God 'with all manner of instruments'. Smaller ensembles occur too, especially in paintings of the Virgin and Child from the late 15th and early 16th centuries.

Fig. 34b. **Lute,** by LAUX MALER, Bologna c.1520. *Kunsthistorisches Museum Vienna.*

Fig. 35. VENETIAN SCHOOL, (c.1500). *The Virgin and Child Enthroned Between Angels.*

Marco Palmezzano's *Virgin Enthroned with SS John the Baptist and Lucy* (fig 34) is a fine example of this genre. The Virgin is enthroned in an architectural setting, holding Jesus and with a landscape in the background. The two saints stand on either side with an angel sitting in front below the Virgin's dias playing a large lute with nine strings. These are evenly spaced, although more usually nine strings would be grouped as four pairs and one single top string, such five 'course' lutes being common at the time. The lute had by this period gained that position of pre-eminence which it was to hold for the next century or so, and it is the instrument most often associated with the Virgin in Renaissance art (fig 34b). The angel is gazing upwards, her mouth slightly open, possibly singing the Virgin's praises to her own accompaniment.

The two angel musicians of another Italian painting of *The Virgin and Child Enthroned Between Angels* (fig 35) by an unknown master of the Venetian School c.1500 are playing not only a lute, here a six course instrument with the strings clearly in pairs except for the usual single top string, but also a recorder. Seated on either side of the Virgin, the two angels in this painting are unlikely to represent an actual musical ensemble for their purpose is to represent the Virgin's supremacy over

Fig. 36. Studio of MARIOTTO ALBERTINELLI. *The Holy Family,* painted c.1500.

both the spiritual and the sensual sides of human nature, represented by the lute and the recorder. This painting has been retouched in later centuries, the rosette on the lute in particular showing evidence of repainting. The recorder, with an uncharacteristically expanded body and large tongue and window, is held unmusically, the player's fingers not over the soundholes, seven of which are visible.

A lute appears again in association with the Virgin in a painting of *The Holy Family* (fig 36) from the studio of Mariotto Albertinelli, also of c. 1500. This shows a change from the formal arrangement of the previous paintings to a freer and more human treatment. Mary and Joseph are seated in a landscape with Christ and another child playing in front of them. Behind, an angel plays a lute, the neck of which is hidden.

A painting by the Piedmontese artist Pietro Grammorseo of *The Immaculate Conception* (fig 37), dated 1526 and stylistically more akin to the German than to the Italian school, emphasises the contrasting symbolism of stringed and wind instruments. The Virgin is kneeling in prayer, surrounded by clouds and cherubs with some of the Old

Fig. 37. PIETRO GRAMMORSEO. *The Immaculate Conception,* dated 1526.

Fig. 37a. detail.

Fig. 37b. **Rebec and Bow,** from SEBASTIAN VIRDUNG. *Musica Getutscht.* (Basel, 1511).

Testament metaphors mostly from the 'Song of Songs', which were applied to the Virgin of the Immaculate Conception. God the Father looks down from above and at her feet two angel musicians play stringed instruments. The angel on the left plays a lira da braccio, the noblest instrument of the period, here with three melody strings, three corresponding pegs on the pegbox, and a drone string running beside the fingerboard. This drone string is attached to a short peg sticking out unusually and probably incorrectly at right angles from the neck and not from the pegbox itself. This angel barely touches the bow with the tips of her fingers in a scarcely credible hold. The angel on the right plays a strikingly decorated rebec with a carved animal head. The rebec was a bowed three-stringed instrument with a pear-shaped

Fig. 38a.　detail.

Fig. 38.　LUDOVICO MAZZOLINO. *Pharaoh and his Host Overwhelmed in the Red Sea*, dated 1521.

body hollowed from a single piece of wood. Although especially used for dance music, evolving during the 16th century into the 'kit' or dancing master's fiddle, the fine decoration on this instrument suggests a nobler role than the profanity of dance.

This lower portion of the painting is unfinished. Between the two angel musicians can be seen the wings of a third angel, a largely blank area, and an open book, which suggest an uncompleted angel (or angels) singing from music. The Virgin is sometimes portrayed in 16th century art in her role as predestined to bring about the redemption of man from the 'sin of Eve'. She may stand over a serpent or other symbol of Satan. Here Satan is portrayed by a man playing a pipe beneath the clouds on which the Virgin kneels and in dark shadow which contrasts with the brightly lit angel musicians directly in front. This clearly shows the contrasting symbolism of stringed instruments for the Virgin and wind instruments for Satan. Though largely hidden, the pipe is clearly of the flageolet type, of which the most characteristic example at the time was the tabor pipe which was fingered with one hand while the other hand beat a drum slung around the player's waist.

Fig. 39.   JEROME FRANCKEN I. *The Marriage Feast at Cana.*

Fig. 39a.   detail.

The 'pipe and tabor' ensemble first appeared in the 12th century and was known throughout Europe in the 16th century. It usually appears in pictures played by soldiers and by itinerant musicians.

In the above paintings musical instruments have all been, as it were, consciously included: a painting of the Virgin and Child or of the Holy family will not necessarily include musicians, but where one does their presence is of significance. Paintings of biblical scenes, as distinct from devotional portraits such as of the Virgin and Child, became increasingly popular during the Renaissance. In these, contemporary life is reflected so that musicians may occur simply because their presence would be normal in the Renaissance in a context such as that of the biblical scene portrayed. Thus, in Mazzolino's *Pharaoh and his Host Overwhelmed in the Red Sea* (fig 38) dated 1521 two flageolet players and a drummer can be seen amongst the crowd of Israelites on the right hand side of the painting (fig 38a detail). The flageolet resembles the recorder but has a narrower body and was mainly associated with popular music.

Two biblical banqueting scenes in the National Gallery Collection are Jerome Francken I's *Marriage Feast at Cana* (fig 39) of the late 16th century, and Willem van Herp's *Herod and Salome* (fig 40) which dates from the mid 17th century. In Francken's painting, one of a number of almost identical paintings by various artists in different collections, the

Fig. 40. WILLEM VAN HERP. *Herod and Salome.*

Fig. 40a. detail.

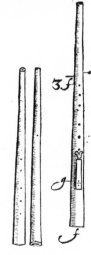

Fig. 40b. **Mute Cornetts,** from MICHAEL PRAETORIUS, *Syntagma Musicum II, De Organographia,* (Wolfenbüttel, 1619-1620).

musicians who stand in a gallery at the back of the banqueting hall comprise three lutenists, one woodwind player (possibly a recorder, though it could be a reed instrument), and a boy singer, a characteristic ensemble for indoor music in the later Renaissance in Flanders. In Herp's painting however, we see in the musicians, as in the setting and the dress of some of the diners, a mixture of the contemporary and the antique. The musicians here are two singers who hold a book of music, and two instrumentalists. One plays a straight wind instrument of uncertain identity, possibly a mute cornett, an important Renaissance instrument still in use in the mid-seventeenth century (fig 40b). The second instrumentalist is playing a lyre of antique design, not an instrument in use at the time the painting was made.

The *Triumph of David* (fig 41), from the studio of Guercino (early 17th century), has a musical content explicit from the Old Testament: 'When David was returned from the slaughter of the Philistine . . . the women came out of all cities of Israel singing and dancing . . . with tabrets, with joy, and with instruments of music' (1. Samuel 18;6). Holding the head of Goliath, David is accompanied by lady musicians.

50

Fig. 41.   Studio of GUERCINO. *The Triumph of David.*

One plays a small kettledrum suspended on a strap around her shoulder, two play tambourines, and two sing from a sheet of music on which can be seen a portion of the biblical text *'et David decem millia'* ('Saul hath slain his thousands, *and David his ten thousands'*).

Turning from paintings of biblical subjects to those of the saints we find that these are not often portrayed with musical connections since the attributes which identify the saints and their settings are largely predetermined and music seldom features. One of the exceptions is St. Francis who in paintings of the Counter Reformation is sometimes accompanied by angel musicians. David Teniers the Younger's *Ecstasy of St. Francis* (fig 42) shows the saint, identified by his attributes of a crucifix and skull, in a landscape, with an angel in the sky playing a violin. The details of the violin are unclear, but its respectability for a religious subject is confirmed in this context.

No series of religious paintings with musical connections would be complete without the patron saint of music, St. Cecilia. A virgin martyr of the 2nd or 3rd century, Cecilia was honoured as a saint from early times, but her connections with music only evolved during the

Fig. 42. DAVID TENIERS THE YOUNGER. *The Ecstasy of St. Francis.*

15th century. One of the most famous paintings of her as patroness of music is by Raphael (in San Petronio, Bologna) of which there is a copy attributed to Domenichino in the National Gallery (fig 43). This painting is most interesting because most of the many musical instruments which lie at her feet, which include recorders, triangles, small kettledrums, cymbals, and a viol, as well as her attribute, a portative organ which she holds uncaring and upside down, are broken

Fig. 43. Attributed to DOMENICHINO, After Raphael. *The Ecstasy of St. Cecilia.*

Fig. 44a. **Harpsichord** by DOMENICO DA PESARO, Italian, 1590. *National Museum of Ireland.*

Fig. 44. JACOPO VIGNALI. *St. Cecilia.*

or damaged. The explanation is that, looking up to heaven and listening to a choir of angels, she is rejecting the profane music of the world, represented by the broken musical instruments, in favour of the music of the angels. Her portative organ is also unusual in that it is portrayed back to front, the longer bass pipes at the right hand end of the keyboard not the left.

A second painting probably of *St. Cecilia* (fig 44) is by Jacopo Vignali (formerly attributed to Carlo Cignani), and dates from the early 17th century. By this period the portative organ, formerly the saint's traditional attribute, had dropped out of general usage and she is shown instead playing a harpsichord in concert with two angels playing a large lute and singing. It is the presence of these angel musicians who identify the saint. The harpsichord is a characteristic

Italian instrument of the period (fig 44a), with single manual, decorated outer case, and resting on a table rather than on its own legs. Beside it lies a tuning key. The lute played by one angel is a theorboed lute, having six lower bass strings off the fingerboard and attached to a second pegbox (not visible here), and twelve pegs representing six double courses on the main pegbox.

5 Music, Myth, and Morals

SCENES OF CLASSICAL mythology, and cupids, satyrs and fauns, are a feature of renaissance and baroque art. When musical instruments appear in these paintings they may be imaginary and unrelated to reality, or they may be actual musical instruments, whether antique or contemporary with the artist, but which often carry a symbolic meaning beyond their musical function. The use of musical instruments as symbols also occurs in other paintings, in particular in the Dutch School in the 17th century where they may contribute to an often complex moral allegory.

One of the characteristic instruments of Ancient Greece and Rome was the double aulos or tibia, a reed instrument whose distinctive shape of two divergent pipes was well known to artists of the Renaissance and Baroque from surviving classical sculpture. One appears in an oval painting of *Putti at Play* (fig 45) in imitation of a classical bas-relief, by the late 18th century Flemish artist Peter de Gree, and by its very presence emphasises the classical nature of the subject. More often than not however putti and other classical figures play instruments which are not related to reality, such as fantastically curled or serpentine 'trumpets' not based on any real models, as in Johannes van Haansbergen's *Classical Landscape* (figs 46 and 46a).

In a painting of *Bacchanalian Boys* (fig 47) of the 17th century Neapolitan school, six naked boys play out of doors. In front of them on the ground lies a large tambourine or frame drum and a woodwind instrument of uncertain type. The association of a tambourine with Bacchus himself occurs in a painting of the story of *Bacchus and Ariadne* (fig 48) by François de Troy. Ariadne rests out of doors as the young Bacchus arrives to wake her, holding his ivy entwined thyrsus and

Fig. 45. PETER DE GREE. *Putti at Play.*

accompanied by a maenad, one of his female devotees, playing a tambourine. In the foreground are a satyr and a second maenad. The use of tambourines and drums by the maenads who accompany Bacchus derives from the ancient rites of Dionysius in which women played drums and tambourines. Thus in the Neapolitan painting of the bacchanalian boys the tambourine, even when lying unplayed in the foreground, identifies the boys as bacchantes. The sensuality of wind instruments is also appropriate to Bacchus, and in the *Triumph of Bacchus* (fig 49) of the school of Rubens the music is provided by a satyr on the left playing a shawm-like instrument.

Cupid is the subject of countless paintings of the Baroque. One of the many themes with which he is associated is that of Love the Conqueror, or Love Triumphant, in which the power of love over other emotions and activities is portrayed, or of pure love over carnal lust. In the latter case lust may be represented by a satyr as in a 17th century painting after Annibale Carracci called *Omnia Vincit Amor* (fig 50). On the right in a sylvan setting are two nymphs, and on the left a

Fig. 46. JOHANNES VAN HAANSBERGEN. *A Classical Landscape.*

Fig. 46a. detail.

Fig. 47.   NEAPOLITAN SCHOOL,
(17th CENTURY). *Bacchanalian Boys.*

Fig. 48.   FRANÇOIS DE TROY. *Bacchus and Ariadne.*

59

satyr, or Pan himself, who kneels in submission to Cupid who clutches his horns as a symbol of love subduing lust, in defence of chaste love represented by the nymphs. On the ground in front of the satyr lies a set of panpipes, their sensual and passionate music silenced by Cupid.

The origin of the panpies is related by Ovid: Pan was pursuing the nymph Syrinx who found her escape cut off by a river. She prayed to be transformed to escape from Pan who, reaching out to grasp her, found himself clutching a bundle of reeds. The wind blowing through the reeds made a sound which so delighted Pan that he cut them to make a set of pipes, the panpipes. They are sometimes known by the name of the nymph Syrinx. Pan being a symbol of carnal lust, the panpipes themselves are one of the strongest musical symbols of the widespread association of wind instruments with the passionate side of human nature which we have encountered in other contexts. In Paolo Fiammingo's *Feast of the Gods* (fig 50) Pan, sitting on the ground near the banquet table, is again identified by his pipes.

Another mythological figure who is associated with panpipes, again as a symbol of lust, is the one-eyed giant Polyphemus who loved Galatea the sea-nymph, who was herself in love with the youth Acis.

Fig. 49. School of PETER PAUL RUBENS. *The Triumph of Bacchus.*

Fig. 49a. detail.

Fig. 50. **After** ANNIBALE CARRACCI. *Omnia Vincit Amor.*

Nicolas Poussin's painting of *Acis and Galatea* (fig 52) shows the couple in each other's arms with nereids and cupids in attendance and a triton playing a conch shell, the musical symbol of the sea, while on a rock behind, Polyphemus disconsolately plays his panpipes.

Returning to the theme of *Love Triumphant,* there is a 17th century painting including musical instruments attributed to Orazio Riminaldi (fig 53), one of a number of paintings in different collections by lesser artists who were inspired by a similar painting by Caravaggio. Cupid is shown here standing in triumph over various objects representing aspects of human life and achievement: war is symbolised by armour, knowledge by books, painting and sculpture by palette, brushes and a piece of sculpture and sculptor's tools, mathematics by dividers, set square and books of geometry, exploration — one of the peaks of man's achievements in the early 17th century — by sextant and armillary sphere, and music by musical instruments and books of music. These musical instruments are placed at the opposite side of the painting to the armour, for music is itself the opposite of war.

Fig. 51. PAOLO FIAMMINGO. *The Feast of the Gods.*

Fig. 51a. detail.

Fig. 52. NICOLAS POUSSIN. *Acis and Galatea.*

Fig. 52a. detail.

Fig. 53a. **Cittern,** Italian 17th century.
Ashmolean Museum, Oxford.

Fig. 53. Attributed to ORAZIO RIMINALDI. *Love Triumphant.*

Fig. 54. BARTOLOMMEO BETTERA. *A Still-Life.*

The instruments shown are three important stringed instruments of the period. In front lie a lute and a violin. The lute has thirteen strings arranged in eight courses, the bottom two and the top one having single strings, and there are seven frets. The top string is intentionally shown broken, for it symbolises the power of music conquered by love. The violin is characteristic of the time with its early form of bridge, tailpiece of light-coloured wood, and short neck. At the back is a large cittern, a plucked instrument with metal strings in contrast to the gut strings of the lute. Where the neck joins the body can be seen the distinctive shoulders which are the atrophic and non-functional vestiges of the arms of the ancient lyre from which the cittern ultimately derived (fig 53a).

Apart from the figure of Cupid, Riminaldi's painting is essentially a still-life. A noted Italian painter of still-lives from the same period is Bartolommeo Bettera, by whom the Gallery has a *Still-Life* (fig 54) which includes again three stringed instruments amongst other objects. The instruments are a large lute, which is largely hidden, a mandora, related to the lute but smaller and with a sickle-shaped pegbox carrying five strings in this case, and a violin with its bow. An open book of music is also shown.

Dutch and Flemish paintings of the 17th century often portray moral allegories, and the presence of musical instruments, as of other objects, may be largely symbolic. In Willem Duyster's *Interior with Figures* (fig 55) five people are standing or sitting around a table on which rest a lute, the pegbox with eighteen pegs towards the front, and a violin largely hidden but with the relatively flat tailpiece of pale-coloured wood visible. On the left of the table is an elderly couple, the lady dressed in black, the gentleman in a more flamboyant colour, and behind the table are two youths. One of the youths is flamboyantly dressed and drinks from a glass, while holding a wine jug with the other hand, representing worldly pleasures and excess. In contrast to him the other youth is dressed more soberly.

On the right of the picture a young lady, also dressed respectably with black dress and broad ruff collar, plays a lute which, with its ability to play quiet, harmonic music, is a symbol of concord and temperence. This lute is identical to the one on the table. In addition to the contrast between the excess of the wine-drinking youth and the temperence of the lutenist and the other youth, this painting contrasts youth and age. The lute and violin on the table in the centre of the group serve to bring harmony and unity into the opposing lives of excess and of temperence, and between youth and old age.

Musical instruments fulfil a similar passive symbolic role in another 17th century Dutch *Interior with Figures* (fig 56) by Thomas de Keyser, a painting which is an allegory of love and marriage. In the centre of the room a young lady sits in front of a fire, one foot resting

Fig. 55. WILLEM DUYSTER. *An Interior with Figures*, or *The Five Senses*.

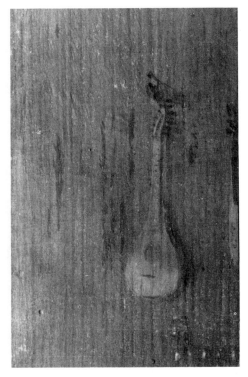

Fig. 56a. detail.

Fig. 56. THOMAS DE KEYSER. *An Interior with Figures.*

on a foot warmer, symbolising the warmth of love. Behind her, holding the back of her chair, stands her lover or fiancé. One of the strongest allusions to marriage occurs in the statue of a naked lady on the near side of the fireplace. The peacock beside her identifies this lady as Juno, protectress of women and especially of marriage and childbirth. On the other side of the hearth, in which burns a fire which can both symbolise the ardour of love and act as a test of faith and of innocence, is a statue of Jupiter, the faithless husband of Juno, identified by the eagle he holds. Thus the two lovers are faced with a powerful allegory of marriage in which the centre, love, is flanked on the one side by a warning of the risks of infidelity in the form of Jupiter, but on the other by the happily more prominent, protective figure of Juno.

In a painting portraying such strong symbols it is hardly possible that anything should be included which does not contribute in some way to the allegory. So what are the three musical instruments doing in the rear left of the painting? Hanging on a wall are a dancing master's kit and a cittern, two instruments associated with profane pleasures. The kit (fig 56b), a relative of the violin but with a very narrow body to enable it to be carried about in a dancing master's coat pocket, was widely used for dance music in the 17th and 18th centuries. The cittern, which also featured in Manetti's *Love Triumphant*, enjoyed widespread popularity but was representative of the lower levels of society. In the words of the German musician and writer Michael Praetorius, author of the most extensive late renaissance book on musical instruments (published in North Germany in 1619) the cittern was 'almost an ignoble instrument, used by cobblers and barbers'. Traditionally citterns were hung up in barber's shops for the use of the waiting customers. Lying on a table in front of these two instruments is a violin, whose musical context at this period was still largely that of dance music. Thus we have three contemporary instruments all suggestive of profane pleasures, and even, in the Calvanist moral atmosphere of the time, directly of sin. It is important that these are rejected by the couple contemplating marriage, who have literally turned their backs on them, leaving them untouched in the furthest and darkest corner of the room.

The inclusion of musical instruments for their symbolic content in portraits was encountered in Mytens' portrait of a *Lady Playing a Lute* and Troost's *The Dilettanti* in Chapter 3.

Paintings such as these Dutch examples can be misleading when using pictures as a basis for the reconstruction of past performance practices. By their very realism and accuracy of detail they may appear to provide an almost photographic record of instruments in their everyday settings, when in reality the instruments may have been chosen for extra-musical reasons quite unrelated to their actual musical or even social setting.

Fig. 56b. **Kit,** by JACQUES DUMESNIL, Paris 1647, *Victoria and Albert Museum, London.*

6 Irish Music

BECAUSE OF THEIR choice of subject matter, Irish paintings prior to the 19th century rarely reflect the music of the people. However, amongst the portraits of the earlier 18th century is Francis Bindon's small painting of the great blind harpist Turlough O'Carolan (fig 57 shows an engraving of this portrait). This portrait may have been commissioned by one of the families in whose country houses O'Carolan enjoyed patronage and hospitality, for of all native Irish musicians of that period it was O'Carolan who came closest to bridging the divide between the native musical traditions and the imported tastes of the wealthy minority. This portrait shows O'Carolan playing his harp, only part of which is visible. Another famous harper was Arthur O'Neill who played at the Belfast Harpers Festival in 1792. In 1760 he played the so-called Brian Boru harp in the streets of Limerick (this harp is now in Trinity College, Dublin, fig 57a). A portrait by Conn O'Donnell (fig 58) shows him playing, elegantly dressed as he always was.

During the 18th century music flourished in Dublin on a scale unparalleled until our own times, and the fashionable rather than the native musical tastes are reflected in paintings of the period. The Irish peer Lord Charlemont is shown playing a recorder in a group caricature painting (fig 28) by Joshua Reynolds, an instrument also played by Nathaniel Hone the Elder's son in a portrait, *The Piping Boy* (fig 59) dated 1769 in which the recorder has a rounded mouthpiece rather than the usual beaked type. Charles Jervas's portrait of *Lady Mary Wortley-Montague with a Clavicytherium* (fig 26) features a fanciful clavicytherium or upright harpsichord, an instrument known to have been made in Dublin in the mid 18th century, although it must be born

CAROLAN,
The Celebrated Irish Bard.

_ To His Excellency the Marquess Wellesley, K.G.

LORD LIEUTENANT of IRELAND &c &c

Fig. 57a. **Irish Harp, Probably 14th century.**
Trinity College, Dublin.

Fig. 57. FRANCIS BINDON. *Turlough O'Carolan (1670-1738).* Line and Stipple
engraving by John Martyn, 1822.

70

Fig. 58. CONN O'DONNELL. *Art O'Neill,*
(1737-1816).

in mind that Jervas's painting is based on an earlier Italian painting (see
Chapter 3) and so is not necessarily representative of an Irish
instrument.

Another Irish portrait from the early years of the 19th century by
George Chinnery (fig 60) shows *Mrs. Conyngham* sitting at a piano (or
possibly harpsichord) and at her left elbow sheets of music on a table

Fig. 59. NATHANIEL
HONE THE ELDER.
The Piping Boy,
(Camillus, son of the
artist), dated 1769.

Fig. 60. GEORGE CHINNERY.
Mrs Conyngham.

Fig. 60a. **Apollo Lyre,**
English c.1800. *National
Museum of Ireland.*

Fig. 61. GEORGE JOSEPH. *Sir John Andrew Stevenson (1761-1833).*

against which leans a fine lyre guitar, a form of guitar modelled on the shape of the ancient classical lyre and which enjoyed a wide vogue during this period. The particular model shown was known as an 'Apollo lyre' after the medallion of Apollo's head visible at the top of the instrument, which hinged back to give access to the tuning pegs (fig 60a). Also dating from the early 19th century is a portrait by George Joseph of the composer *John Stevenson*, (fig 61) born in Dublin in 1761

Fig. 62.   ENGLISH SCHOOL, (19th CENTURY).
*Thomas Moore (1779-1852) in his Study at
Sloperton Cottage.*

and who died at Kells in County Meath in 1833. Associated with both
Dublin cathedrals, he wrote mainly church and theatre music but is
best remembered today as the editor and arranger of the music for
Moore's *Irish Melodies.*

With the 19th century painters in Ireland as elsewhere turned
increasingly towards subjects taken from everyday life. Interest in the
folk music of Ireland was also growing, and collections of folk tunes
began to appear. Such collections formed the basis of Thomas Moore's
Irish Melodies which themselves contributed to the popularisation of
Irish traditional music. A portrait by an anonymous English artist of
Thomas Moore in his Study (fig 62) includes an Irish harp resting on the
floor near a square piano, the precursor of the modern upright piano.
The two instruments represent the two sides of Moore's music: the
harp as the instrument of the traditional musicians from whom his
tunes derived, the square piano as the characteristic instrument of the
drawing rooms for which Moore made his arrangements. The

Fig. 63. JAMES HARWOOD. *Samuel Lover (1797-1868).*

National Gallery also has portraits of Moore by William Essex, John Jackson, Daniel Maclise, George Mulvany, and Martin Shee. Another nineteenth century portrait with a piano in the background is the painting by James Harwood of the author, artist and musician *Samuel Lover* (fig 63). A copy of his song 'Father Connel' lies in the foreground.

Of all paintings of Irish music and musicians, Joseph Haverty's *The Blind Piper* (fig 64) must be one of the best known. It is a portrait of

Fig. 64. JOSEPH HAVERTY. *The Blind Piper,* painted c.1844.

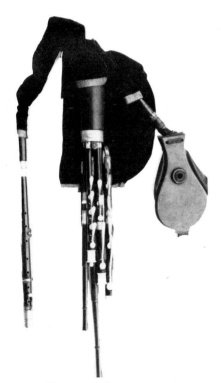

Fig. 64a. **Uillean Pipes** by O'FARRELL. (engraved on instrument: 'O'Farrell's Union Pipes'), Irish c.1800. *National Museum of Ireland.*

Padraig O'Brien who was born in County Clare c.1773 and became a street musician in Limerick. There Haverty painted him with his daughter sitting beside him, romanticising the setting by representing him in a wooded landscape rather than against a background of the

Fig. 66a. detail.

Fig. 65. THOMAS BRIDGFORD. *An Irish Piper*, painted c.1843.

streets of Limerick. The uillean pipes, or union pipes, are a form of pipes peculiar to Ireland which are bellows blown with drone pipes some of which, known as regulators, can be altered in pitch while playing. They were at the height of their popularity at this time and some fine examples dating from the late 18th and early 19th centuries exist in the National Museum of Ireland and other collections. It is difficult to distinguish the precise number of drones and regulators on

Fig. 66b. detail.

Fig. 66. DANIEL MACLISE. *The Marriage of Princess Aoife of Leinster with Richard de Clare, Earl of Pembroke (Strongbow),* painted c.1854.

Fig. 67. DANIEL MACLISE. *Merry Christmas in the Baron's Hall,* dated 1838.

the instrument in this painting, but two long drone pipes are clear and there are probably two, maybe three, regulators.

Another portrait of an uillean piper from the mid 19th century is by Thomas Bridgford (fig 65), in which the piper poses with his instrument which he is not playing. The bellows attached to the player's arm, by which the instrument is sounded, can be clearly seen, but the chanter is held in his right hand.

The 19th century romantic view of Ireland's past, in which music is represented by the Irish harp, appears in Daniel Maclise's *Marriage of Aoife and Strongbow* (fig 6), a painting in which the political implications of the marriage for the future of the country are symbolised by a bard with an Irish harp, some of whose strings are broken, and who is surrounded by dead people and others sleeping. In the background three soldiers play imaginary curled brass horns based by Maclise on ancient models, together with two more anachronistic brass instruments reminiscent of those in the modern orchestra, including a trombone. Another painting by Maclise, *Merry Christmas in the Baron's*

Fig. 67a. detail.

Fig. 67b. detail.

Hall (fig 67) also shows a romanticised scene from the past, including musicians some of whose instruments, like those of the previous painting, are not historically accurate.

Paintings with traditional music-making are quite rare, but mention should be made of Trevor Fowler's *Children Dancing at a Crossroads* (fig 68), dating from the mid 19th century, in which the children dance to music played by a boy with a wind instrument of uncertain identity. It is shown end on, the only distinguishable feature being a broad bell at the lower end of the instrument, a feature not found on any instruments associated with Irish traditional music. The most usual small wind instrument over the last century or so, and probably the one which Fowler was thinking of but depicted incorrectly, has been the tin whistle or penny whistle. In the foreground of

Fig. 68. TREVOR FOWLER. *Children Dancing at a Crossroads.*

Walter Osborne's view of *St. Patrick's Close, Dublin* (fig 69), painted at the end of the 19th century, a boy plays a tin whistle. Of all paintings of musical interest this perhaps best reflects music in its everyday setting, the young boy playing for his own enjoyment or perhaps to earn some pennies from passers by.

Child musicians, or children pretending to be musicians, feature in Richard Moynan's large painting *Military Manoeuvres* (fig 70) dated 1891. The scene is a street in the then small rural town of Leixlip with a group of boys pretending to be soldiers marching. Some are playing real or pretend instruments: a penny whistle similar to that in Osborne's painting, a small keyless flute or fife, a biscuit tin and a bucket serving as drums, saucepan lids as cymbals, a metal coffee pot blown through the spout as a cornet or trumpet, and a second 'trumpet' in the form of a folded paper tube.

An interesting record of a real military band from earlier in **the** century is provided by William Turner de Lond's painting of the *Entry of King George IV into Dublin in 1821* (fig 71). The royal procession is passing through a triumphal arch in front of the Rotunda and is headed by a

Fig. 69. WALTER OSBORNE. *St. Patrick's Close, Dublin,* dated 1887.

Fig. 70. RICHARD MOYNAN. *Military Manoeuvres,* dated 1891.

Fig. 71b. **Trombone,** by Robinson, Bussell & Co., Dublin c.1850 stamped with the British Coat of Arms. *National Museum of Ireland.*

Fig. 71c. **Serpent,** by THOMAS KEY, early 19th century. *National Museum of Ireland.*

band of cavalry musicians. In front is a mounted timpanist, and behind follow the band riding four abreast and playing trumpets, trombones, horns, serpents (a bass wind instrument widely used in military music well into the 19th century), bassoons, bass drums, and a jingling johnny which is an ornamental pole with small bells hanging from it which was introduced into European bands from Turkey in the early 19th century. (Another painting of the same ceremony by Joseph Haverty shows the procession in front of the Bank of Ireland building, but the band is not shown).

Music as part of a ceremony appears too in John Sherwin's oil sketch of the *Installation Banquet of the Knights of St. Patrick* held in Dublin Castle in 1783. The detail is poor, but a choir, organ and two trumpeters can be made out on the balcony at the back of the hall. An engraving by Sherwin of the same scene (fig 72), of which the National Gallery also has several versions, shows a mixed band of instruments. Some of these, including horn players, can just be discerned in the oil sketch, overpainted by the choir and organ.

Fig. 71. WILLIAM TURNER DE LOND.
George IV, King of England, Entering Dublin in 1821.

Fig. 71a. detail.

Fig. 72. JOHN KEYES SHERWIN. *The Installation Banquet, in Dublin Castle, of the Knights of St. Patrick, 1783.* Line Engraving by the artist, 1803.

Dublin musicians in the late 19th and 20th centuries, including amateur musicians, feature in a number of paintings. These include a portrait by Louis Werner (d. 1901) of the cellist *Professor W. Elsner* (fig 73). His cello is without the normal spike to support it on the floor, the absence of which was an old-fashioned feature of Prof. Elsner's technique for which he was noted. On a table beside him rests a score of a 'concerto for Violincello and Piano, opus 3' apparently by Brahms, although the composer's name is partially obscured by a music stand and moreover Brahms wrote no concerto for cello and piano, his op. 3 being a set of solo songs.

A portrait by Sarah Harrison, dated 1926, shows *Michele Esposito* (fig 74) holding some of his own music. Esposito was born in Naples in 1855 and came to Dublin in 1882, where he soon made his mark as a pianist, teacher, and composer. For nearly half a century he dominated musical life in Dublin, and founded the Dublin Orchestral Society

Fig. 73. LOUIS WERNER. *Professor W. Elsner (1826-1884).*

Fig. 74. SARAH HARRISON. *Michele Esposito (1855-1929),* dated 1926.

which was the only organisation putting on orchestral music in Dublin in the early part of this century. He left Dublin in 1928 to live in Florence where he died the following year. Walter Osborne's *Portrait of a Lady* (fig 75) shows Mrs. Caesar Litton Falkiner sitting at a piano.

The Rehearsal, (fig 76) by an unknown Irish artist of the 19th century, shows a group of musicians; one man stands and conducts at a table at which sit a flautist and two singers, with a fourth man listening. A cello and sheets of music lie in the right hand corner.

Of more recent date is Sean Keating's *Homage to Frans Hals* (fig 77),

Fig. 75.   WALTER OSBORNE.
Mrs. Caesar Litton Falkiner.

Fig. 76. IRISH SCHOOL, (19th CENTURY). *The Rehearsal.*

a light-hearted portrait of Sean Nolan, City Sheriff of Dublin and a noted traditional fiddler who died in 1955. He is shown in evening dress holding his violin in a parody of Frans Hals's portrait of a man playing a lute, which hangs on the wall behind him.

Fig. 77. SEÁN KEATING. *Homage to Frans Hals; A Portrait of Sean Nolan, (1897-1955).*

SELECTED BIBLIOGRAPHY

Major sources and literature relating to paintings discussed in this book, in addition to suggestions for further reading.

BAINES, Anthony, *European and American Musical Instruments* (London 1966)

BOYDELL, Barra, *Sounds Tempting* An Aspect of Musical Iconography, in: *Irish Arts Review* (Summer 1985) Vol 2 No 2. *The Installation Banquet of the Knights of St. Patrick*, in: Dublin Historical Record XXXVI/3 (1983)

BROWN, Howard Mayer, & LASCELLE, Joan, Musical Iconography (Cambridge (Mass.) 1972)

FORD, Terence, *Andrea Sacchi's Apollo Crowning the Singer Marc Antonio Pasqualini*, in: Early Music 12/1 (1984)

HALL, James, *Dictionary of Subjects and Symbols in Art* (London 1974)

HAWARD, Lawrence, *Music in painting* (London 1945)

LEPPERT, Richard, *Arcadia at Versailles. Nobel Amateur Musicians and their Musettes and Hurdy-gurdies at the French Court (c.1660-1789)* (Amsterdam and Lisse 1978). *Concert in a House – Musical Iconography and Musical Thought*, in: Early Music VII/I (1979)

PRAETORIUS, Michael, *Syntagma Musicum II, De Organographia* (Wolfenbüttel 1619-1620; R/Kassel 1976)

MERSENNE, Marin, *Harmonie Universelle* (Paris 1633: R/Paris 1963). National Gallery of Ireland.
National Gallery of Ireland, Illustrated Summary Catalogue of Paintings (Dublin 1981)

REMNANT, Mary, *Musical Instruments of the West* (London 1978)

SADIE (ed.) *New Grove Dictionary of Musical Instruments.*

WINTERNITZ, Emanuel, *Musical Instruments and their Symbolism in Western Art* (New Haven and London 1979)

Continental and British Schools

Column groups: **PERCUSSION** (triangle–drum) · **STRINGS** (lyre–violin) · **WIND** (uncertain brass–double aulos)

School	toy instrument	singer	piano	harpsichord	organ	triangle	jingling Johnny	tambourine	drum	lyre	Irish harp	guitar	mandora	cittern	lute	hurdy-gurdy	lira da braccio	kit/pochette	rebec	medieval vielle	viol	basse de violon	double bass	cello	viola	violin	uncertain brass	uncertain woodwind	conch-shell	trombone	horn	trumpet	bagpipes, bellows-blown	bagpipes, mouth-blown	serpent	cornett	bassoon	oboe	shawm	flageolet recorder	flute	panpipes	double aulos
Albertinelli, Studio of (1100)															1																												
Bazzani, Giuseppe (982)																															1												
Bega, Cornelis (28)		2																							1																		
Bettera, Bartolommeo (1014)												1		1												1																	
Biondo, Giovanni del (943)					1																1																						
Bolognese School, see After Carracci, Annibale (1078)																																											1
Brueghel the Younger, Pieter (911)																																		2									
After Carracci (1078)																																											
Cignani, see Vignali (183)																																											
Coster, Adam de (1005)	1																																										
Couture, Thomas (4221CB)																																1											
Coypel, Attr. to Noel (1656)																													1														
David, Jacques Louis (4060)																															2												
De Gree, Peter (1106)																																											1
Diano, Giacinto (357)																																									3		
Domenichino attr. to (Raphael copy) (70)		6			1	1			2											1																							
Dusart, Cornelis (324)																1																											
Dutch School, see After Teniers the Younger (1694)																																											
Duyster, Willem (333)														2											1																		
English School (19th cent.) (4312)		1								1																																	
Fiammingo, Paolo (1834)																																									1		
Flemish School (16th cent.) (1049)		2																																									
Florentine School (15th cent.) (780)								1																								1				1							
Francken I, Jerome (4094)		1												3																1													
Grammorseo, Pietro (771)		1?															1	1																		1							
Guercino, Studio of (1323)		2?						2	1																																		
Haansbergen, Johannes van (341)																															2												
Herp, Willem van (1082)	2																																			?							
Hogarth, William (792)				1					1																																		
Hondt, Hendrick de (512)								1																							1												
Honthorst, attr. to Gerrit van (1379)															1																												
Kamper, Godart (806)																									1																		
Kauffman, Angelica (200)				1																																							
Keyser, Thomas de (469)													1					1							1																		
Lebel, Jean (721)																1																											
Lebel, Jean (722)		3																							?	2														1			
Lemaire, Jean (800)																																										1	
Lippi, Attr. to Filippino (470)														1		2																								?			
Lorme, Anthonie de (516)																															1												

94

PERCUSSION — STRINGS — WIND

	toy instrument	singer	piano	harpsichord	organ	triangle	jingling Johnny	tambourine	drum	lyre	Irish harp	guitar	mandora	cittern	lute	hurdy-gurdy	lira da braccio	kit pochette	rebec	medieval vielle	viol	basse de violon	double bass	cello	viola	violin	uncertain brass	uncertain woodwind	conch-shell	trombone	horn	trumpet	bagpipes, bellows-blown	bagpipes, mouth-blown	serpent	cornett	bassoon	oboe	shawm	flageolet/recorder	flute	panpipes	double aulos
Lundens, Gerrit (1033)									1																								1						2?				
Marchand, Jean (1260)		4?							6																																		
Mazo, Juan del (659)								1	1			1																															
Mazzolino, Ludovico (666)									1																														2				
Meissonier, Ernest (4261CB)															1																												
Meulen Adam van der & Bout, Peeter (1713)																1																											
Molenaer, Jan (1529)																																		1									
Mytens, Jan (150)															1																												
Neapolitan School (1074)								1																					1														
Ostade, Adriaen van (32)		3																																									
Palmezzano, Marco (117)															1																												
Passeri, Giovanni (993)								1				1																															
Pater, Jean-Baptiste (730)																								1									1										
Pater, Jean-Baptiste (731)									1																															1			
Poussin, Nicolas (814)																														1													1
Poussin, Nicolas (816)																																											1
Quillard, Pierre (546)															1					?	?					1																	
Raphael copy, see Domenichino (70)																																											
Rembrandt, School of (439)																										1																	
Reynolds, Joshua (734)																									1																1	1	
Reynolds, Joshua (737)																									1																1	1	
Riminaldi, Attr. to Orazio														1	1											1																	
Roslin, Alexandre (1824)																										1																	
Rubens, School of (1064)																															1							?					?
Ruisdael, Salomon van (507)																																	1										
Schiffer, Matthias (1886)																								1	?	3				2							2	2					
Sherwin, John (396)					1																									2													
Teniers the Younger, After David (1694)		2										?									1																						
Teniers the Younger, David (1655)																														1													
Teniers the Younger & Uden, Lucas van (41)																																		1									
Troost, Cornelis (497)																																									1		
Troy, François de (723)								1																																			
Turner de Lond, William (1148)							1		4																		2			2	2	4			2	2							
Van Dyck, After (1372)																																											
Venetian School (c.1500) (480)															1																												
Vierpyl, Jan (1025)				1																																							
Vignali, Jacopo (183)		2		1											1																												
Watteau, Follower of (801)												1																															
Werner, Louis (4115)																								1																			
Wheatley, Francis (125)									1																																		

95

	toy instrument	singer	piano	harpsichord	organ	PERCUSSION triangle	jingling Johnny	tambourine	drum	STRINGS lyre	Irish harp	guitar	mandora	cittern	lute	hurdy-gurdy	lira da braccio	kit/pochette	rebec	medieval vielle	viol	basse de violon	double bass	cello	viola	violin	WIND uncertain brass	uncertain woodwind	conch-shell	trombone	horn	trumpet	bagpipes, bellows-blown	bagpipes, mouth-blown	serpent	cornett	bassoon	oboe	shawm	flageolet/recorder	flute	panpipes	double aulos
Irish School																																												
Bindon, Francis (1344)											1																																
Bridgford, Thomas (855)																																	1										
Chinnery, George (837)			1	?						1																																	
Fowler, Trevor (4122)																												1															
Grogan, Nathaniel (4074)																															1												
Harwood, James (142)																																1											
Haverty, Joseph (166)																																1											
Hone the Elder, Nathaniel (440)																																									1		
Howard, Hugh (773)																																									1		
Irish School (19th century) 1818																								1																	1		
Jervas, Charles (4342)					1																																						
Keating, Seán (4196)															1										1																		
Lavery, John (1644)		1																																									
Maclise, Daniel (156)		2						1	1																	1				1		1				1		2					
Maclise, Daniel (205)											1																4				1	1											
Moynan, Richard (4364)	5																																			1				1	1		
Mulready, William (387)	1																																										
O'Donnell, Conn (1200)											1																																
Osborne, Walter (836)																																									1		
Osborne, Walter (1060)		1																																									
Osborne, see Irish School (1818)		2																						1																	1		
Russell, George (AE) (4071)										1																																	
Russell, George (AE) (4105)										1																																	
Russell, George (AE) (4106)																																											
Russell, George (AE) (4111)										1																																	
Paintings of musicians without instruments																																											
Harrison, Sarah (1219)																																											
Jackson, John (257)																																											
Joseph, George (416)																																											
Maclise, Daniel (4054)																																											
Mulvany, George (1097)																																											
Shee, Martin (775)																																											